Restoring Sacred Art

Restoring Sacred Art

JOSEPH BATHANTI

Restoring Sacred Art
© 2010 by Joseph Bathanti

cover art: *Exaltation* by Philip DeLucia

Cover design: Trisha Hadley

All rights reserved. No part of this book may be used or reproduced in any manner whatsoever without written permission from the publisher, except in the case of brief quotations embodied in articles and reviews.

Published by

~Star Cloud Press®~
6137 East Mescal Street
Scottsdale, Arizona 85254-5418

ISBN:
978-1-932842-39-5 (cloth) — $ 24.95

978-1-932842-40-1 (paper) — $ 14.95

Library of Congress Control Number: 2010921212

Printed in the United States of America

OTHER BOOKS BY JOSEPH BATHANTI

POETRY

Communion Partners
Anson County
The Feast of All Saints
This Metal
Land of Amnesia

SHORT FICTION

The High Heart

NOVELS

East Liberty
Coventry

NONFICTION

They Changed the State: The Legacy of North Carolina's Visiting Artists, 1971-1995

Acknowledgments

Many thanks to the following publications in which some of these poems originally appeared, occasionally in different versions: "Sandlot" in *Aethlon*; "Wheeling" in *Asheville Poetry Review*; "The Cameraphone" in *Cold Mountain Review*; "Sainthood" in *Explorations: the 20th Century*; "Eggplant" in *Italian Americana*; "Joe-Joe" in *The Literary Review*; "Rapunzel" in *The Madison Review*; "A Dream of the Dead on Good Friday" in *North Carolina Literary Review*; "Nobody's Child" in *Pembroke Magazine*; "Every Good Boy Deserves Favor" in *Pennsylvania English*; "Restoring Sacred Art" in *The Pittsburgh Quarterly*; "Chronic Pain" in *Rivendell*; "The Last Time I Drank with Phil" in *The Recorder*; "Practicing Love" in *Seattle Review*; "Face of Fire" in *South Carolina Review*; "Shoplifting" and "The Tongue" in *Tar River Poetry*; "Collins Avenue," "Dog Eat Dog," and "The Dryer" in *VIA: Voices in Italian Americana*; "Sister Jane Evelyn" in *The Wallace Stevens Journal*; "Wrestling," "Your Leaving," "The Curse," and "Domenico Giuseppe" in *West Branch*.

"Dog Eat Dog" won the 1999 Aniello Lauri Award from *VIA: Voices in Italian Americana*.

"Restoring Sacred Art" won the 2002 Sara Henderson Hay Prize from *The Pittsburgh Quarterly*.

"The Dryer" and "Collins Avenue" won the 2006 Aniello Lauri Award from *VIA: Voices in Italian Americana*

The poem "Knocked" was published by the Pennsylvania Center for the Book as one of its featured poster poems for the PUBLIC POETRY PROJECT in 2010.

for
Jacob and Beckett

Table of Contents

Face of Fire	1
The Tongue	5
Son of a Bitch	8
Penance	10
Sister Jane Evelyn	14
Carsick	17
A Dream of the Dead on Good Friday	20
Sainthood	22
The Electrifying Vernacular of Escape	26
Every Good Boy Deserves Favor	28
The Cameraphone	30
Shoplifting	32
Rapunzel	35
Collins Avenue	37
Silence	39
Wrestling	41
Joe-Joe	44
Wheeling	48
Knocked	52
Swimming in the Allegheny	54
Not Talking	57
Your Leaving	61
Sandlot	64
Dog Eat Dog	67
The Dryer	69

The Curse	74
The Last Time I Drank with Phil	77
Nobody's Child	78
Chronic Pain	80
Eggplant	83
For My Mother on her 76th Birthday	84
The Orange	85
Practicing Love	90
Bitter	92
The Future	95
Maria Rosalina	99
Domenico Giuseppe	102
My Father's Hat	105
Restoring Sacred Art	106

Face of Fire

I knew Fred Houk was a drunk.
He had a whiskey nose, swollen,
pin-pricked, pomegranate pink
with a cleft in its middle
as if he'd stood too long with it
pressed against the black iron fence stiles
that kept us penned in the schoolyard.

As he hunched by, toting a burlap
of rat pellets and jug of disinfectant,
I could smell it on him.
Like the huckster's touched fruit
fermenting in the truck bed, sickly sweet,
the flies sluggish and drunk
sucking its rot.

Indentured to some unnamable sin,
the nuns said he couldn't talk,
as if one of the church statues
had come to life and donned the grey habit
of a janitor, his mop and snow shovel,
the thick black, cracked leather belt
with its shackle of haunted keys.

Joseph Bathanti

He became for us Levitical,
a hair-shirted hermit hatching out
his private penance, brewing
fire in the incinerator room
where he kept a hotplate,
a Winchester racked on a hammered row
of rusty ten-pennies,
and his plaid thermos of Rye.

All eight grades mustered for his Requiem.
In the second, I had never been to a funeral.
God sent gothic weather to fit the occasion.
The benighted stained glass drooped and scowled.
From their chains, three stories above us,
the chandeliers strangled.
Saints Peter and Paul, the parish namesakes,
cowed in their alcoves above the celebrant,
Father Battung, a German Jesuit,
who cut his Scotch with milk to coat his ulcer.
His vestments were black,
a dayglow cross on his chest;
and on the breast of Fred's coffin,
the same crest. Mrs. Houk,
throughout the Mass, screamed:
"Freddie, Freddie, oh my God, Freddie."

So much like the martyrs was his death
I imagined him in his hellbox a monster.
Dead drunk, my mother had said.
How else could he have managed
to pitch out of bed and lay all night
with his face melting against
the searing steam register?

Listening to Mrs. Houk rave,
I couldn't get out of my head *Face of Fire*,
a horror matinee I was cajoled
into by older boys about a man
whose face had been burned so hideously
he hid it under a black cowl.
But there was that moment in the movie
when he lifted it off, just one
split frame of his gooey cauterized stare.
The image annealed in my psyche like Jesus's
face in Veronica's veil.

I tore out of the theatre,
home to nightmares of that countenance
mooning over my bedstead, blowing
its Purgatorial breath in my face.
Face of fire. Fred Houk's face
in that coffin up on the altar,
his widow going on and on, "Freddie,
oh, Freddie, Freddie," as if instead of dead,

Joseph Bathanti

    he were merely lost, until shivering
    we closed our eyes and covered our ears
    and even the nuns held hands.

The Tongue

> *And the tongue is a fire,*
> *a world of iniquity.*
> — St. James 3:5

My mother used to threaten with her death.
I won't live to see this or that
or simply, *I'll be dead.*
A child, sure I had sown her death wish,
I was terrified of these utterances.

But with each day,
I learned what a liar was the tongue,
how it culled vendetta,
then fell silent. Busy bricking
myself into a tomb to rival hers,
I thought, *Go ahead and die,*
but stop talking about it.

One day when she was dressing –
we had to pay bills and I was furious
about going – I turned and said
inside the ruined temple of my head,
fuck, a word, like love, I didn't know
the meaning of, but felt like nails,
blood-real, not word-real –
like the fact of fire.

Joseph Bathanti

I'd thought I'd been talking to myself,
but the sound of that word –
cheap, weightless, thrilling –
wormed out of me in a voice
which the house over and over whispered back.
In only her underthings,
my mother wheeled, clutched for cover
a towel to her throat and breast
in a gesture I would see
astonished women forever copy.

Unable to deny it,
I stood outside her bedroom door,
the tip of the word still hanging
like a switchblade from my mouth.
Suddenly, to punish her for the shame I felt,
I wanted to be dead.
I knew that clipped syllable had amounted
to the confession I had been secretly making
to myself minute by minute
every day of my life.

I couldn't possibly have known
all those years ago – I was just a little boy –
what that word meant.
Looking at my mother as she backed mutely

into her room and out of my life –
as if she were about to crash unclothed
through the window into the snowstorm,
leaving me once and for all –
it was clear
she too was innocent of it.

Son of a Bitch

Johhnny Petro's dad, Al, was a *son of a bitch*.
His fellow coaches, including my father,
had no use for him. Excluded,
red-faced, he looked like Lee Harvey Oswald.

"Get in front of it," Al commanded,
forbidding Johhny to flinch
as he clubbed him vicious grounders
with his big Hillerich and Bradsby 35,
a cigarette stealing out of his mouth like a bullet,
the ball tearing rabid along the mined field.
"Take it in your chest.
What are you afraid of?"

My father had known Al for years,
but said little aside from the times, often enough,
when Al crucified Johnny because of a boot
or strike out. My dad would tell him to let up,
and Al would wheel menacingly,
then smile when he saw who it was.

I thought it took something secret
to brand a man *son of a bitch*:
murder, or sins of impurity.
More than baseball, more than fathering

a boy who couldn't catch, had no arm,
no swing; a boy smart enough
("Too smart," Al would mutter)
to realize there was no future in 1963
on that glassy, pocked field
down on Larimer Avenue.

"Are you a statue?" Al would bellow
in the middle of an inning
when a ball shot by Johnny,
then mimic his son, standing motionless,
head hanging, arms drooped at his sides,
the two of them identical, still as marble,
except for the boy's squint behind his glasses.

Joseph Bathanti

Penance

Frantic with relief,
like a child fished from a well,
I burst from my First Confession
into the sunlit world, how kind now

that I was finally good. Upon my tongue
the next morning I would accept
another sacrament, Holy Eucharist,
and become the bones of slaughtered saints

immured in glass reliquaries,
all light and sweet decay.
It was fine to die.
Headed home, I strayed

into a pickup game in Booze Alley:
cobblestones, a hideless, unravelling ball;
cracked bat hammered with finishing nails,
wrapped in sticky electrical tape.

The black kids from Hilliards,
they didn't wear shirts.
Their hair was tiny.
Geraldine Gumto, the street tomboy,

who would become a nun.
And Jacky Lando. *Little Jack.*
No bigger than a toy, but cruel and foul-mouthed,
daredevil, dark-skinned.

Wearing a moldy unstrung glove he found
climbing Goodwin's garage roof,
he could catch anything.
The adults said he was headed for trouble.

Through the flume of sanctifying grace
enclosing me, I saw it too:
Jacky's bent toward evil glory
flaming, like one of the bad angels.

We argued: *safe* or *out*.
He fired slag in my face,
remanding me for a blind instant to pitch and fear.
Sin grouted inside my eyelids.

I threw a wild punch,
opened my gravelly eyes, and saw the others
frozen in wonder:
Jacky soughed a crown of blood at my feet.

Joseph Bathanti

> Then from his mouth slipped a pearl,
> and then another and another
> dropping like fantastic alms onto the alley floor,
> as if my fist, guided by the Holy Spirit,
>
> had split a secret vault of treasure in him.
> The other children backed away,
> as if I were the bad one. Jacky howled
> like judgment, blood bearding him,
>
> dripping from his chin, and I knew
> that my Confession had been annulled.
> Jesus would refuse my tainted heart.
> Dipping my hands into the dirt,
>
> scooping up his blood and teeth,
> sun and silvery filth coating them,
> I knelt and offered them to him,
> as if he were the Prince of Peace,
>
> the very least of them.
> It was in His power to call back His blood,
> resow His teeth, spin time back
> to the moment outside the confessional

when my soul was spotless. But instead,
looking down at me upon my knees,
he marshaled his principalities,
his wiles and discernment,

cried piteously
like a wounded little boy,
then spit his wild suffering
blood in my face.

Joseph Bathanti

Sister Jane Evelyn

> *She said poetry and apotheosis are one.*
> *"A Pastoral Nun"*
> —*Wallace Stevens*

No memorable thrashing,
not even the words, wormy
now with disuse, that she shot me with
when I was too clever and erred,

the trickle of nouns, as I read from my primer,
spilling from my mouth,
staining my white uniform blouse
and little blue necktie.

She'd lick the star I hated,
my prize for knowing too much,
and press it between my eyes.
She was more beautiful

than the Blessed Mother,
beauty never called by its name,
but withheld like necessary praise
for the gaudy child about to weep in the corner.

How I loved her.
To punish me,
she would make of herself a cross,
arms at right angles from her body,

the feathery habit swooping wrist to waist
like raven pinions I would enter
and have closed upon me.
Disappeared, chrysalid, I'd wait

in the darkness for her voice,
my lips against her husband's cruciform
lounging at her breast.
Talc was all the Order permitted,

but she wore it like allure,
the dense broadcloth subsuming me
as she squeezed and whispered,
"The word and the will of God are one,"

which meant nothing to me,
being not of language, but of thingness.
I knew that if I inched further
I would enter her nun-flesh

and, like the tarantula bridegroom,
I must die.
So I stilled myself until she preened
and I was released to my battered desk

in its row of tittering stares
until she called on me to read again.
I gazed down at the page of vowels
and consonants roiling like chromosomes

in the concupiscent world of Mother and Father
and their gleaming progeny, Dick and Jane.
What would bring me to
was her impatience,

the wedding band rapping off the chalkboard
behind which I imagined a trapped boy
who had imprinted on his forehead
the gold star of the Phonics champion.

Carsick

As soon as my father gets home from the mill,
we hurry to pick up my mother
who has hunched for eight hours
over a sewing machine
in what she calls the *sweat shop*.
Hers is a dying trade.
The only woman in men's alterations,
she feels her otherness, honing
her hate like a basting knife
for the *greenhorns just off the boat*.

It's dusk, gray as gargoyles,
salt and slush battering the Belair
as it clings to McKnight Road's icy curves.
Along with me in the backseat,
pressed against her window, my sister
Marie reads until my father tells her it's too dark;
then she stares at the black trees and headlights.

The inside of the car crowds with shadows.
Night outside our machine
becomes a remote conversation overheard.
Tucked into my corner with a pillow
and army blanket, I'm too sick to say
what it is; but I scratch
with my finger on the seat beside me
the story I must live inside

Joseph Bathanti

until this ride is over.
My father's cigarette moves in an arc
from his mouth to the ashtray
until he throws it out the window,
hawks and spits, and lights another.

We park in front of Gimbel's and wait
like we do every night until my mother
is in the car and we are back
on the slick black highway.
She tells my father about her day:
What they said, what she said
to put them in their places,
Calabrese bastards.
He says nothing, jams on the turn signal,
carries me in and lays me on the couch.
My mother sits on the floor beside me
and shows me the stamps that Hymie,
the lone Jew tailor in the shop,
her one friend there, has sent me.
He is deaf and his speech badly slurred –
from the concentration camps.
My mother holds up to me
the tiny squares and rectangles:
kangaroos, Montezuma's ruins,
a volcano in Chile,
Ubangi in the Belgian Congo.

Why does Hymie send me these stamps?
Who writes the letters?
The ones who've escaped it all,
the only trace of them in a foreign language,
their worth measured in exotic currency,
the red postal circle of cancellation
sealing the silence among us all?

My mother has fallen asleep,
still whispering to me that it's alright.
I hear my father in the kitchen,
the pages of Marie's book turning
beside her lamp upstairs,
outside the snow falling.

Joseph Bathanti

A Dream of the Dead on Good Friday

Napping in my grandmother's widowed bed,
I have my first dream of the dead.
My grandfather has lost his paycheck
and is walking, hands clasped behind
his back, along Washington Boulevard.
He never learned American or to drive.
There's a Super 8 clip of him
sliding through the front door on Omega Street.
He was a ghost long before he died.
In the closet still breathing the silent air
choked with mothballs are his few clothes.
He was a hat and sweater
worn by teeth and flint,
hands that said *enough*, or *too much*,
a mouth sealed with whiskey
stubble to keep in the fire.
No one talks about him.
In the dream:
I am with him, my eyes
on the road, searching among all else
that's been lost or forgotten,
for the envelope of money with his name on it.

When I wake, the air raid
siren is caving in the rooftops.
Christ is crossed; and, though the sky
is blue, a storm immanent.
My face has slid from the pillow
to the rosaries my grandmother sleeps with.
The beads bore holes in my cheek.
She speaks French to King
as she lets him into the house,
then Purina clicking into his bowl.
The siren makes him suicidal.
It has happened, especially on Good Friday,
to other dogs in the neighborhood.

The smell of Easter bread, rising
on Omega Street, shrouds the open window.
The silent radio is draped in purple cloth.
The table heaves with loaves
iced in white crosses.
My grandmother works dough with flour and oil.
I go to her, press my face
into her stomach and breathe.
King lies at her feet.
Easter morning he'll disappear;
and my grandmother, in her best
dress and beret, will sit
on the curbstone and weep.

Joseph Bathanti

Sainthood

With apostolic zeal
the nuns made plain that at random
one might be called upon to die for the faith.
Sainthood, they called it, craving
with every breath, they professed,
the opportunity for glory
the headsman occasioned.

I desired sainthood as much as anyone,
but made myself sick obsessing
over what would come for me
at the appointed time, the door
suddenly kicked in by an infidel
demanding I renounce Jesus.

Methods of martyring ranged from simple dispatch –
Venantius was beheaded, Mathias stoned –
to the peevishly imaginative:
Saint James was *hurled down*
from the terrace of the temple
and clubbed to death,
the Forty Holy Martyrs exposed on a frozen pond,
Bartholemew flayed alive.
The North American martyrs,

Isaac Jogues and the other mad Jesuits,
suffered fingers and toes chewed off by the Huron.
Still conscious, they watched their organs eaten.

At tiny desks we crayoned
coloring-book sketches of them
in our Catechism Primers,
imagining what kinds of martyrdom
North America would require of us.
Crayola red for blood.
"Stay within the lines," the sisters commanded.

At night, catacombed in bedclothes,
I argued with myself.
Of course I would die for Jesus:
ten days agony, broken glass, snakes,
molten ore, vivisection.
But why not hoodwink my inquisitors?
Simply feed them white lies:
that I was through with Jesus,
I'd worship Baal or Apollo.
To placate them,
to get them to call off the big cats
and put up those blunt rusted instruments.
God would know
that in my heart I hadn't betrayed Him.
Why be tortured and die?
I was only seven.

Joseph Bathanti

But, in that same heart, I knew:
Only blood and agony could dye
the royal robes of sainthood;
only death could wear its crown.
There was no *no* when they came for you,
no *yes*. Only death,
and you had to be happy about it.
The martyrs sang praises as they expired.
Further I'd hunker under the covers,
fingering into the bedsheet
the shape of a fish,
then pray to disappear.

In your sleep lions sound like a bed
dragged across a wooden floor.
The vibrato, ineffable power
gathering breath; and pretty soon
it's inside you. Roaring,
but so much bigger, distant
and large as the ocean,
yet in the house, padding
down the linoleumed hall.

I suppose I got scared and screamed
because my parents would be there,
telling me it was just a dream;

and the three of us would listen
to the lions' caged rumbling.
We lived just two blocks from the Pittsburgh Zoo.
"You've heard them since you were born,"
they reasoned. The way they smiled
at me as if they knew something.
I'd think, maybe finally it's all over.
Maybe I'm in heaven.

Joseph Bathanti

The Electrifying Vernacular of Escape

As a girl, Marie read so much
my mother branded her lazy,
a withering accusation in our house
of ceaseless toil. In her way,
Mother was a Calvinist.
She believed in mortifying the flesh,
denaturing will.
Work took your mind off things.
It's nothing, she liked to say of our discomfort.
Just thank God you have both arms and legs.

Each page Marie turned,
each flight of make-believe,
described a stray footprint on the carpet,
a dirty saucer on the sideboard,
the newspaper left overlong on the ottoman.
Words possessed a focused untidiness,
immodest, black as Negroes,
violating the pristine doily of the page.

My sister, pale, bespectacled,
disarrayed cross her bed, a book
like an infant splayed in her arm,
terrified my mother; as if
in her incessant reading she had authored
Mother against her will: cursed
and unforgivable, lashed

to keeping a house where words like mice
burst from the woodwork,
tumbled among the silver, dropping
behind them the punctuation of regret,
the bitter trope of memory.

Adhering to vows of silence and obedience,
Marie said nothing.
She would close her book,
clip its place with a holy card of the Virgin,
press dutifully through the house,
like a captive forced to char,
scouring porcelain, mopping linoleum,
redding soiled linen from the beds,
whatever homage the raised octaves of my mother required.

Yet that book, like a forbidden lover,
whispered from its hiding place,
luring her back to it with promises
of seduction and danger:
the electrifying vernacular of escape.
It was just a matter of time before she slipped
into its pages and disappeared.

Joseph Bathanti

Every Good Boy Deserves Favor

For Sister Mary Lawrence

Along with the bonnet of charity,
she took the name of the martyr, Lawrence,
roasted on a gridiron over slow fire.

She taught us music.
When she was sent away after finally cracking,
flogging herself with a songbook,

we bragged we had driven her to Mayview.
Her mistake was kindness: no beating,
no screaming, but Chopin and Mozart.

We made her pay for our singing,
braying for spite the *Tantum Ergo*,
ball-pointing our initials into her adored piano.

On the other side of the room,
the girls tried to drown us
with their heavenly sopranos.

But their puberty was no match for ours.
In black leather, we were killers.
It was too late for a truce with Lawrence's Order.

Their sticks had sanctified our meanness.
About to cry, she'd pick away the wire
spectacles imbedded in her face

and with a handkerchief wipe
at the grooves around her pink eyes.
This is when I would stop in my heart

savaging her, though the rest of me
went on with the others.
She'd grow morose, the black pitch pipe

stabbing out of her black habit,
her voice still beautiful, falling,
falling as she sang. Mumbling

the Beatitudes, she'd look off
like a ravaged bride, offering it up,
making a gift of us to God.

Joseph Bathanti

The Cameraphone

The infamous East Liberty adult theatre

Its very name to me was sin,
the marquis emblazoned with the naked
alphabet jutting over the sidewalk.
Too young to read the titles,

nevertheless I knew.
We never walked that side of the street;
and I dared not chance a peek,
so insistent was my mother's white-

gloved hand around mine as she, tight-lipped,
snubbing the very air she breathed,
towed me along Penn Avenue.
But I had another eye (for desire)

that saw as though through scrim,
past the bored, over-lipsticked old woman
in her flesh-colored ticket booth
into the smoky lobby where men gathered

silently in darkness in the middle of the day,
not looking at one another,
but shuffling down aisles to sit alone
in the perfect pitch of their torment.

On screen flashed the writhing white things
men long all their lives to see
and end up paying for,
something back in their innocence

they might have called love
had they been able to speak of it.
Instead they took wives, and fathered,
remained in their ways good, silent

till the end, even on their deathbeds
unable to confess, certain
they must burn in hell –
and I, too, for having imagined them.

Like soldiering, or driving a car every day
to a mill job or taking out the garbage,
I knew these things only in the most distant way –
that some day I would have to be one of them.

Joseph Bathanti

Shoplifting

The traffic cop on Penn Avenue wore white gloves
and smiled at us. In navy blue blazers,
saddle shoes and ties emblazoned
with the Mater Dolorosa, we crossed

in the safety of his outspread wings,
on our way to rob National Record Mart.
Already in our duffle bags were cupcakes
and cigarettes from A & P.

Only one clerk, a teenager
in corduroy velour elephant bells
and yellow granny glasses.
On the store turntable played *Paint It Black*.

From their racks, the one-eyed 45s glared.
Our parents moonlighted
so we could attend parochial schools
and make something of ourselves.

Their best boast was that no one
in the family had ever gone to jail,
but I would find out later
this was a lie.

I had a premonition of everything narrowing,
the air sucked from the room
like prelude to a cyclone,
the huge sidewalk windows darkening

with scrutiny, the Stones' gyrating fury,
the cop's silver whistle
screeching above the car horns.
The trick was to take

what you really didn't need,
exploit the moment of inattention,
that maudlin flicker stealing
across the shopkeeper's lips

like an old song, unable to stop
himself from being somewhere else,
the pressed, black acetate in the sun-beads
blinding him while we hid in vials

of light, taking from the world
what it wouldn't give willingly.
At night I laid on ironed sheets, listening
over and over to Wayne Fontana

and the Mindbenders' *A Groovy Kind of Love*,
singing along: *When I'm feeling blue,*
all I have to do is take a look at you.
Then I'm not so blue.

That seemed about perfect.
But I had no love.
Boys like me turned into punks,
sent to Morganza and Thorn Hill,

then Hell. Too afraid to confess a real sin,
like the guy in the song, I couldn't
control the quivering inside.
That was the only record I kept.

The others I sailed – black saucers –
off Larimer Bridge and watched them
shatter off the boulevard
four hundred feet below.

RAPUNZEL

Her bedroom was in the turret
of the lavish Tudor.
It had a window of Tiffany
I imagined her levering open
one night as I careened home
down Bryant's long hill,
my bike stuttering off its buckling
Belgian block, and calling my name,
her gown dropped
off her shoulders, her hair
a ladder of honey dripped over
the brick trellice for my climb.

I found myself in that room only once,
with the rest of my class
when we were taken to visit
by Sister Saint John of the Cross.
My Rapunzel had somehow fallen
from her watchtower
and broken her back.
She lay in a body cast,
her beauty like a saint's,
finally immured in plaster,

Joseph Bathanti

a huge metal handle
like those used for hoisting a trunk
sticking out of it, her hair
chopped off like a nun's.

COLLINS AVENUE

The nights of tripe and bocci
they hobbled down to Troiano's saloon,
dragging like chained shades behind them
lives shipped in steerage
across the Atlantic,
artifact hands working like marionettes,
coarse operatic garments
of self-loathing and insane pride,
headstone faces inscribed
with gold teeth, concrete skin
we expected any minute would chip away
and reveal a monster with a shrill,
superstitious wife given to rosaries
in dark churches.

All evening behind the clubyard wall
we heard Vivaldi's sonata,
Al Santo Sepolcro, revving and dying
over and over on the windup Victrola,
the querulous wooden crack of the balls
and voices like the creak
of a crowbar unprying the rusted-shut.

Joseph Bathanti

They didn't own the words to articulate
their wounds, not even in their native tongue,
though we, the children, *Americanos*,
could not have comprehended.
They belonged to us, these old men,
and we to them; but we had no old country,
only Collins Avenue, this one *via*
along the pinched breast of a new country
they could not turn their mouths from.
America had murdered Christ all over again.

Doomed to haunt the family *fotografie:*
no names, averted faces,
flashing gunbore eyes,
canes and crutches propped
against the Quince tree, rising
arm after arm with its mutant fruit,
under which they brooded, hoarding
their damnable secrets like blood money.

Spare is my translation.

Silence

> *Silence is a family trait.*
> *Some ancestor of ours must have been a solitary man –*
> *a great man surrounded by halfwits, or a poor, crazy fool –*
> *to teach his descendants such silence.*
> — Cesare Pavese
> —"South Seas"

Denying there is in me sleep
I lay in the cool cotton deep
of my grandmother's otherworldly bed
that smells of lilies and freshly scrubbed flesh.
Sycamore racemes, just come
to fruit, paw the window,
fanning sunbursts over my sheets.
A lost boy on a spotless keep,
I do not dream, but am dreamt,
sure my eyes have never closed;
yet the tree has bent across the room
an hour of its shadow, the light,
in a conical gleam like a movie ray,
now on the white porcelain doorknob,
turning until released, revealing
in its naked jamb my dead tailor grandfather
in a suit of invisible smoke.
He walks, lock-jawed, hands hidden
at his back, to my bedside,
and looks down slowly.

Joseph Bathanti

>
> His gray face grinds open. Finally,
> finally he is speaking to me.
> I try to rise to the sound of it,
> but I am stillborn, pinned in Limbo,
> unnamed. What is he saying?
> I can't make it out.
> Then he turns his back,
> his snubbed hands sewn to each other.

Wrestling

Coach Big Jim hums *Blue Moon*
while he cracks my back,
then puts his Bassett hound forehead against mine
and tells me, "Take him, Joey."

In the middle of the black mat,
my opponent and I shake hands
as is customary and I make the mistake
of looking into his face.

Famished, tired,
I had spent two tournament nights,
three overtime periods too many,
crouping over the mat-side bucket of blood

and hawkers after outlasting some other
starveling whose blood sugar had finally
dropped a notch below mine and lapsed
into the narcosis of the impervious

gym rafter lights and all I had to do
was fall over on him. I was dreaming
of the food I had packed,
an array of dainties:

Joseph Bathanti

tortes and kirsches, flans, crepes. Imagine.
Yet among wrestlers such narcissism,
cupidity, really, is not uncommon.
I lived by the mirror, carried in my book bag

a bathroom scale, weighed my spit and excrement,
ate only citrus and iceberg, no water.
Only a week ago I had beaten this same boy,
locked him in a cradle the last two minutes,

but couldn't get the ref to bring his hand down.
Tonight he wants me in an inconsolable way.
No one had ever taken him before.
His nerves are shot;

he smells of booze and Romilar.
But so are mine – vertigo, the shakes,
mild hallucinations, the teeth-grinding
lust for two shots of bourbon and a cigarette.

Somewhere inside hesitation is a tripwire:
a flinch at the takedown, an aborted
Fireman's Carry, letting the other boy
read your mind. It would be easy,

even cliché, to call this loss.
It's so sudden, nothing to be done
about it; but try to believe it's you,
crying – Big Jim, now singing

very softly, or so you imagine,
"I saw you standing alone,"
coming out to walk you back to the bench –
and you're still thinking of sweets.

Joseph Bathanti

JOE-JOE

It's late, late in the game.
We're playing Canevin in our gym,
a bandbox, so small the people
sitting on the bottom bleachers
squat to keep their feet off the in-bounds.

Less than twenty seconds and Central's down one.
Joe Costanzo's bringing the ball up.
Coach Killian's on his feet;
every kid in the school can do
an imitation of his voice.

Joe-Joe loves having the ball,
can't keep his hands off it, really,
and the outside shot is his trope –
a kind of two-hand, knock-kneed jumper,
but he never actually gets off the floor,
the ball with a lot of arc
leaving his hands which twist counter-clockwise,
giving it a reverse english
as it snaps through the hoop,
the net cracking like a stick,
then turns itself inside-out
and the ref has to get it back down
by throwing the ball up
through the underside of the rim.

Joe shoots a lot, more than he has to,
but he can score. On a good night,
he hardly misses.
He'll throw in forty, fifty.
He's captain, All-Catholic,
totally conscious of every move he makes.
He's invented himself and pulled it off.
You can see it when the team comes out to warm up,
the way he swoops in for his lay-ups
as *Sweet Georgia Brown* blares over the P.A.
and Central's tiny gym begins to rock.
Joe's a sweet guy, no denying.
Number 44 in your program,
number one in your heart,
he signs everyone's yearbook.
His dad's a bartender.

The clock shows fifteen seconds.
There's time to work it in
to one of the big guys for something close,
draw the foul: two from the line,
at least one and one.
Tie it up. Overtime.
Play the percentages.

Joseph Bathanti

>
> Canevin's working a half-court man-press,
> so they pick up at center court,
> Joe-Joe right in the middle of the jump circle,
> dribbling, the clock dwindling
> when Russ Benko, one of Joe's boyhood friends
> from Saint Rosalia's in Greenfield –
> everyone's standing now, banging the bleachers
> with their heels, the whole gym literally
> vibrating, the walls sweating –
> Russ yells in his best Mr. Killian imitation.
> There's nobody better at it.
> You'd think it was him.
> His wife would think it was him.
> Russ yells, "Shoot it, Joe-Joe, shoot it."
> And Joe-Joe, at dead half court
> with a guy all over him, never hesitates,
> just throws it up with that quirky twist,
> way up, the ball seeming to spin
> in six different directions.
>
> Killian can't believe it.
> Bending over and beating his thighs with his fists,
> squeezing his head between his hands.
> He's going to kill Joe-Joe.

A cockeyed half-court jumper
with a man open under the boards.
Jesus.

That goes in without touching the rim,
as if there were no rim,
just an invisible hole in the air
that only Joe-Joe and the ball know about,
the net there simply to swoon
like lace on its halo
of orange steel.

Joseph Bathanti

WHEELING

Driving a girl whose father loathed me,
son of an Italian who labored on the open hearth,
I crossed in a borrowed green Comet
the PA line into Wheeling.

Eighteen was legal in West Virginia:
Marlboros and three-two beer at the Hilltop
on a street with whorehouses and a Jesuit college.
She was sixteen, a minor –

the true miners secreted in black sulphurous pockets
whispering beneath the tavern floor we sat upon.
The jukebox was loud and country;
it was easy to ignore the charge being laced under us.

My girl was drunk and singing along – Loretta Lynn,
Tammy Wynette – though she didn't know the words,
the way folks mouth like speaking in tongues
when the spirit lays hold of them.

A smudge on her cheek,
second-hand coat, her blonde hair shone white –
in that light,
aged into a coal miner's wife

or a steel worker's
like my mother.
When the 4 to12 shift from Wheeling Pittsburgh
dragged in, I smelled asbestos

and baked ore, the vaporous green sizzle
of my father's work fatigues.
I wanted to tell her all about her father;
I'd rip him to pieces, that bastard.

My dad was a brave man.
He climbed boom cranes with nothing
but a span of leather fastening him
above the smokestacks streaming

twelve stories of fire into the firmament.
But I had no vocabulary to render his mythic toil.
I knew more about her dad:
his suits and office in downtown Pittsburgh,

his perfect diction and college education.
We hung around till Last Call,
then kissed against the fender
until the lot emptied

Joseph Bathanti

    and the Hilltop's neon shingle sputtered out.
    The Comet wouldn't start.
    I turned it over and over
    until I killed the battery,

    till I couldn't get a peep out of the horn
    or the lights to flicker.
    The mighty Ohio beat by.
     Whelped in Pittsburgh,

    it loops north, in defiance of gravity,
    abruptly slices west, southering
    into the fang of northern West Virginia
    that impales the border

    of Ohio and Pennsylvania –
    like the long jagged neck of a busted bottle.
    That's where we stood clinging to each other,
    stranded along the omniscient river –

    where I still like to think of us –
    before those miners,
    like escaped Purgatorians,
    burst black and smoldering

through the bottom of our lives,
and she started to cry,
anticipating her father's patrician wrath.
I thought of who I could call –

knowing there was only one man on earth
who would rise out of his exhausted sleep
at the sound of my voice,
like Lazarus, and come running.

Joseph Bathanti

Knocked

I was seventeen before I saw Edgar Thomson –
the steel mill where my father had worked
since he was seventeen –
and only then because I needed his car
for the senior after-prom picnic.
The theme was *Color My World*.

Sleepless, having danced all night,
a furnace of cheap champagne
and still in my tuxedo, I dropped him off
at 7 a.m. in Braddock,
named for a Revolutionary War general,
three bars in every block,
streetlights turned on in the afternoon
so the school kids could see
their ways home through the ore dust.

The mill was blue and corrugated,
rising in shaft after shaft
of smoke that saw-toothed into gray sky.
I never saw its top.
The men in the boom crane cabs
wore hardhats and drank coffee.
They had it knocked, my father said.

But not him. He had to climb
the backs of those monsters.

When I was little and insisted
I wanted to be like him
and work in the mill,
he'd snap, "No, you're not.
You're going to college."
In a few months I really would be
going to college. Working in a steel mill
was the last thing I wanted to do.

My father eased out of the car,
handed me a twenty,
told me to be careful,
pinned on his millwright's badge
and filed into the smoke with the others.
I turned up the radio, dropped the engine
into low for torque and floored it,
sure that in one night
I had had more fun, more love,
more everything than he had had in his life;
and I wanted to get back to it
as fast as I could.

Joseph Bathanti

Swimming in the Allegheny

A concrete abutment from an old barge lock
shelved the river. Out of it stabbed

rusty ingots we used to ladder up the slab
and dive into the God-forbidden, dragged

every mill payday for the one who strayed
from the deadman's shift and traded

his union card for shots and beers
in the wharf bars and left

his ballast on the Allegheny floor.
Occasionally a wooden coffin

from the Quaker Orphanage graveyard
unearthed itself like a splinter

working its way to the surface
and slid down the hill into the river.

I swam with tennis shoes on.
The white rubber rims turned green.

I imagined beneath me a submerged city,
myself impaled on one of its palisades,

like an icon on a popsicle stick,
the patron saint of disobedience.

The Gateway Clipper, with its fleet
of ingénues, pitched us a wake.

The girls at lunch on the quarterdeck
waved to us in our briefs.

We threw them the finger, but for all
they knew we were waving back.

Sunk in the trash-clotted bank
was a '64 Navy Biscayne.

In it lay two hardhats and a woman
in just bra and panties.

The doors sprawled open, and music:
I'm your vehicle.

Joseph Bathanti

I'll take you anywhere you want to go.
When they came out to swim, we split,

drying ourselves in the sulphurous air,
flinging our underpants in the weeds

with all the other ditched clothing.
The sun wore lichen.

Not Talking

Even though my mother did not know
how to drive, had been forbidden
expressly by my father who said she cowboyed,
my sister Marie, only 16,
a brand new driver with a junior license,
could not refuse her
when on Washington Boulevard,
just across from the Highway Patrol Station,
she demanded the wheel.

My father did not like to argue with my mother,
but he was adamant about the car.
During her aborted driving lessons,
riding shotgun, spitting
smoke and flecks of tobacco
from his filterless Camel, he would caution:
"Rose, do you see that car
in front of you? Slow down,
for crying out loud. Rose."

He made her nervous, she said.
The stop, the start.
Trying to control her by keeping her from a license.

Joseph Bathanti

If he could drive, she could.
"Pull over," he'd finally order.
She'd slam it into *Park*, get out,
leaving the Chevy door yawing
into the oncoming lane and walk away.
My father would sigh and throw down his cigarette.
"Rose."
"I'll walk home."
"Rose."
"Don't talk to me."

My father never pounded things or screamed.
He didn't even raise his voice.
But when he was mad,
there was a bristling incredulity about him.
He would gape, then look away,
blowing a funnel of cigarette smoke,
then glance back to see if the offender
had been vaporized,
or at least come to his senses.

When the call came from the Highway Patrol
he stared at the telephone receiver
for a whole minute, daring it to take back
the news, before grinding it
into its cradle; and when he knew it wouldn't,
that reconciliation was futile,
he ran, with me trailing, the whole mile
down Negley Run to Washington Boulevard.

My mother had managed to jump the curb,
throttling the blue Belair 45 degrees
up a hill into a black blind of trees.
She hadn't attempted to brake or veer
out of the crash, but threw her arms
around my sister to shield her,
kissing her, making over her
in that operatic vein disaster inspires
in her whole family when it's too late.
She never even thought to switch off the ignition.

A miracle: there was no way to get a car
through there without smashing into a tree.
They sat like that, in each other's arms,
the engine still running, the car rocking
on the edge of the drop to Saint Peter's
Lutheran Cemetery where my father's mother,
who Marie was named after –
even though my mother had planned to name her Cynthia –
was buried by mistake in 1920,
until state troopers rushed up
and eased them out of the car.

When my father and I got there,
the Belair dangled like a fish
by its nose from the tow truck.
No one said a word.

Joseph Bathanti

At this point my memory shuts down.
My father would have said, *So long
as no one was hurt. That's all
that matters. A car can be replaced.*
But he must have said something else,
maybe later in privacy to my mother:
You nearly killed our daughter.
Would he have chanced such an indictment,
knowing it would be the only thing
my mother would remember,
that the rest of their lives would stretch out
in a long highway of silence?

The truth of what really happened
or what might have been said
to so imperceptibly, yet drastically,
alter our lives, is buried –
just as deeply as my mother's perfect,
forever irretrievable instinct
that day on Washington Boulevard
when she wrapped herself around my sister
to protect her.

And Marie? She would have said nothing;
she would have gotten up the next day
and walked to school. In less than four years
she'd marry and go away.
After the accident, I am told,
things were never the same.

Your Leaving

for Marie

The night before you married,
Pap's godsons from Detroit
got him drunk and I had to help
wrangle him upstairs, so mad

I threatened to punch them.
Married men, cement finishers
with mortar grey hands who spoke
broken English with Michigan accents,

they wore Bermuda shorts, undershirts,
black socks and tennis loafers.
My outrage made them laugh.
A father marrying off his only daughter,

his best girl, after all, is entitled
on the eve of the wedding
to drink as much as he wants.
Pap laughed too,

but he felt sorry for me. Like them,
he figured I was still innocent.
We laid him in my bed.
Mother wouldn't sleep with him,

Joseph Bathanti

    "stupid drunk
    the night before his daughter's wedding."
    She blinked the porch light off and on
    to signal you in from kissing

    your fiancé in his red MG,
    the first Protestant
    to marry into the family.
    No wonder Pap got drunk;

    it was your last night home.
    Your bridesmaids slept over,
    cosmetic kits and high, spun hair,
    spit-curls scotch-taped to their cheeks,

    rustling aqua gowns lounging
    from the mantel on cloth hangars.
    The six of you stayed up all night in muumuus,
    laughing and eating popcorn.

    Downtown, the groom and his ushers cheered
    the strippers at The Edison Hotel.
    I had nowhere to sleep,
    so I crawled into your empty bed, and began

    my apprenticeship as an only child.
    The next day, Pap got up
    and donned his mourning suit.
    The girls descended the porch steps

in single file, heads bowed
over nosegays as the photographer
stilled each for posterity.
And you, only twenty, behind them,

without hesitation, disguised
in wedding dress and veil, perfect
in all the ways a bride desires to be,
the repeated click of the camera

documenting those first irrevocable seconds
of your leaving once and for all,
while upstairs Mother sat on the edge
of her bed, still in a housedress.

Joseph Bathanti

SANDLOT

Early, in lieu of church,
so we'll finish by the Steelers kickoff,
we gather in the gloom.
This time of year in Pittsburgh,
the sun is allowed only twice a month
and never on the Sabbath.

Peabody Field, after a high school
mud game, then three days
at twenty degrees, is a frozen glaze
of volcanic pocks. No hash marks,
the rime won't hold rosin. Crystallized
water, like a broken windshield,
aprons the drinking fountain.

The other team is from West Miflin,
half of them still drunk from Whorehouse Bar
boilermakers under the High-Level Bridge
after twelve to eight turns
at Homestead Steel.
They look like Vikings,
breath smoking from singed beards
under bashed helmets.

None of us is drunk, just hung-over,
passing beer and cigarettes,
duck-taping pants up, smearing Bengay
under our jerseys for heat.
The only spectators: our girls
and their girls, imperiously underdressed,
bruised queens bleachered against the sky.

The game is no game, an excuse to brawl,
the ball too slick to pass;
so it's straight ahead, birdcage to bullring
and double-bar, split nose
and the cursing flap of cardboard
pads that spend spring and summer
dry-rotting in cellars.

Threatened by both coaches,
the moonlighting refs, like convicts
in stripes and ear-lugs, jog the chains
plaintively between the twenties
until the gun ends the nothing-
nothing tie in a snowstorm.

Joseph Bathanti

In the car, on the way to Caprino's
Lounge to watch the game,
still in my gear, I gargle
warm beer to loosen the mouthpiece
frozen in bloody spit to my teeth.
Here and there on the sidewalks,
silent figures hump in the snow,
slugging home from Mass.

Dog Eat Dog

Holy Saturday I'm at Berto's
festa with my father
and his *compadres* celebrating
the breaking of the Lenten fast.

Through the eyes of the too sweet
blue-black homemade *vino*,
the laid table looks like a garden,
the raiment of the palate,

plate upon china plate, wine
purpling the white tablecloth
and white shirts, *marinara*
like blood, the corporeal enigma

of fruit and vegetable, the flesh flesh.
Except for the oaths from outside –
when the bocci balls roll awry
and the whiskey lovers are forced to go dry

until they can skill their balls
against the *polino* –
there is little talk of Christ, perhaps
already quickening behind his stone.

Joseph Bathanti

It is best – the not talking
of these men, each of whom wears
around his neck a cross and the gold horn
to ward off the evil eye.

In the darkened next room,
Berto's blind father sits in front of *Shane*.
His long hair is pale bluish white.
A rosary splays his trowel hands.

Out of his golden eyes fall golden tears.
I think he is praying,
but *Dog eat dog* is what he's saying
in broken English as Alan Ladd

outdraws Jack Palance and leaves him dead
under a pile of hogsheads.
"My old man loves that movie," says Berto.
Then he yells in: "Hey, Papa.

Turn that goddam thing off."
The old man waits until Shane,
beginning to slump in the saddle
from the bullet he took,

the little boy pleading with him
to come back, crests Cemetery Hill.
Then he leans forward, fumbles at the knobs,
and turns off the television.

The Dryer

Mere days after we moved into the first
and last house my parents would ever own,
Mary and Herman, our new neighbors, complained
that our clothes dryer made too much noise.
In the alley we shared between the houses –
the silver purring vent ramming out of our cellar –
my father and Herman argued in Italian,
voices grinding like engines turning over;
Herman throwing up his hand, *Basto,*
meaning not only *enough*, but never again.
Silenzio.
My father raising his hand
and ordering me inside.
And that was it.
My parents stopped speaking to them.

Over the years, as batch after batch
of laundry cycled through the dryer,
Mary and Herman's insulbrick house grew
decrepit, strangled by ivy, while my parents
set aside what they could for improvements:
marble fireplace, awnings, wrought iron,
brickwork. Hedges joining the yard
spiked into trees. Behind them
Herman had a little garden.

Joseph Bathanti

In spring I smelled thyme,
basilico, garlic and *cicoria*, wine
from his mouth as he whistled *Maria*.

Mary was in a wheelchair.
Biggy she called Herman.
Dying of Parkinson's he would totter in
and they'd go at it.
"Don't even look at that house,"
my parents commanded as we listened
to their screaming prayers.
But sometimes in winter, pausing in the alley
to warm myself at the vent's sweet breath,
through the window I'd see Mary,
chrismed gypsy hair, loading a tureen
with brackish porridge brewed of Lourdes water;
Herman propped at the table head,
a napkin jittering in his collar.
Their rooms were like a church bazaar,
icon whirligigs and spinning hoodoo votives,
a Blessed Mother who could spit change
and shake hands, sick-boxes on each wall,
TV and radio cued to Fiji mission pleas,
and shrieks of gibberish from Mary.
One morning I saw her rise from her wheelchair
and walk into another room.

I ran in to tell my parents:
a miracle.
"About as crippled as I am," my mother quipped.
"She's always traipsing around."
"Phony witch," said my dad.

As I grew, I saw myself
reflected in their windows
that grimed over even more after Herman died.
I should have spoken to him.
More than once, I started to.
He would have spoken back.
When he saw me he would smile
and shake like an anxious dog.
But I wouldn't look.
It was my duty to hate him.

The rite of silence is solemn, though capricious.
Old age, a death, or mortal illness can soften it.
With Mary, it might have been widowhood
that humanized her in my parents' eyes.
She took to wheeling herself out on the street to sit.
One day she said hello, and my parents answered.
They'd sit and talk from their porches
about how bad the neighborhood was getting
while kids from the projects marched
the middle of the street toward the zoo.

Joseph Bathanti

They promised one another
that if anything happened,
they'd never sell to blacks.

My mother started taking Mary meals,
but when Mary sent back the dishes
with food she had prepared,
my parents threw it away.
I was long gone by then,
but when I came home my mother
sent me over to pay my respects.
Mary asked about me all the time, she said.
I'd take my children
since I didn't know what to say.

Grey and bloated, in the wheelchair
on the porch, a rosary
around her neck
and one in each hand,
"Joey," she'd rasp, and splay out her arms,
kissing me, pinching my face
and looking deeply into my eyes
as if seeing there someone
she had known for a long time.
I was still afraid of her.
Then she'd hold out her hands to the boys and smile.
Dio vi benedica, she'd say, blessing them.
And when she opened her hands

there was candy
which they knew to thank her for
before running off to explode
white-haired dandelions
in the dryer's hoarse whisper.

By then a *For Sale* sign sniped in my parents' front yard.
The cellar stairs had become too much for Mother.
Sometimes she referred to herself as crippled.
If they ended up selling to blacks – so what?
I led my sons into the kitchen,
scoured their hands in the sink,
took Mary's candy,
and threw it in the garbage.

Joseph Bathanti

The Curse

In Memoriam: Captain Joe Somma and Richard DeNinno

For fifteen years I've carried this clipping
my mother mailed me.
Not for its story of the fire captain
who slipped into the rain-swollen Allegheny
while inspecting 4th of July fireworks
and drowned,
but for the photograph
of his fellow firefighters bearing
in the downpour from the boat
to the waiting van marked *FIRE*
the stretcher with his body.

In the center of the picture,
just above the shrouded hump of the dead man,
is my Uncle Dick, in turnout gear,
but no helmet, like a soldier
who has stepped on a booby trap
and walked away unscathed.
As if tailing his own funeral,
he is certain he has died,
that he himself lay under the wet tarp.
Studying his pathetic stupor,
one can understand the atavist's recoil

at the soul-stealing camera,
how it captures the otherwise hidden
spirit which must remain forever fugitive.
He looks like my mother, his sister,
the same shocked, pouting mouth, about to crumble.
She claims she raised him,
that he was born with a clubfoot.

The summer I was sixteen,
his oldest son, whose face
has transposed itself
over my uncle's in the photograph,
was killed in a military accident.
Eavesdropping on the upstairs phone
I heard my uncle, already gone mad,
tell my mother –
they hadn't been speaking to each other –
about Gary, how she had to hurry;
and she, crying, so tenderly saying his name,
telling him she was on her way;
the grudge postponed
until the inevitable next breach.
Death had made it safe to love again.

On the wharf behind the pall-bearing firemen,
what could my uncle be thinking?
He'd been up all night.
The Coast Guard had dragged the river.

Joseph Bathanti

For thirteen hours divers searched,
only to find the lost man thirty feet
from where the barge had sucked him under.
If asked, my uncle would make a joke,
something flip as if, so far beyond telling
the truth, nothing gets to him.

But his face confesses to the camera.
He has brought all this upon himself,
he believes, every bit of it:
his mother and father, brothers
and sisters, massacred
by their own silence;
his captain and friend;
even his beloved firstborn;
that shackle of blood calling him
to answer in fire for his every trespass.

The longer I stare
the more the men locked in this image
look like my family stumbling
through the rain toward eternity,
refusing to look at or speak to one another,
the Sixth St. Bridge dissolving in fog,
skyscrapers crowned in thunderheads.
Our very own Station of the Cross.

The Last Time I Drank with Phil

I'm drinking
in the Rose Garden
at Mellon Park with Philip.
Out all night, we find ourselves
burnished in the high
dawn of Easter, Sunday
sun dripping yellow plates
from the Sycamore's wet green shade.
Spider webs catacomb
the primrose. Angels
spray from silver fountains.
Goldfinches float above
the sequined lawn.
So much light
we shield our eyes,
like the first mendicants,
two old friends, stumbling
upon the risen Christ,
uplifted emerald
bottles of warm Rolling Rock
igniting.

Joseph Bathanti

Nobody's Child

I hated my mother's slumber,
for when she slept,
I stopped existing.

It was as if she had pricked herself
on a witched bobbin and could be revived
only through the fabulous,

her sewing machine still riveting
along like a tiny locomotive,
black and prosthetically smooth

with its flywheels and gold gothic *Singer*.
She had depended so many sentences
from *When I die* that I took the deepness

of her sleep to be not happily ever after,
but forever; and I would take to her
my sorry kiss.

Nobody's child, she'd call me upon
waking in mid-seam and finding
me moping at her feet.

Even now, when visiting, I stray
into her naps to watch for her
aspiration as I do with my children,

tempted to rouse her, but she needs the rest.
I catch myself looking
in her bedroom mirror – to make sure

I'm still there. I always thought
Narcissus drowned,
but he simply pined away.

Joseph Bathanti

Chronic Pain

All night I listen
to my sleepless mother
get up and down:

doorknobs clicking
as she rises from my father –
his snores like a blast furnace –

and prowls room to room,
checking on my children;
her lips to their cheeks;

toilet flush, stairs' creak,
quiver of the ductwork
as she raises the thermostat;

and finally from the kitchen
the kettle keening.
I could go to her.

She's made an extra cup of tea
for the pain that crouches
just across the table,

chronic (*marked by long duration*),
sipping, so devoted. "You bastard,"
I can hear her ruined spine whisper.

But she will not speak.
Never.
She snubs the pain, lets it

like a dead child grow silence.
Her dishes sound in the sink.
She will not resist bending

to the stray crumb or imagined smudge.
There were days when I wouldn't let up on her
and she'd bluff calls to juvenile court,

dialing the numbers slowly,
giving me a look that said,
You have driven me to this.

I could easily turn away
from this poem, deny it,
never return to it.

Joseph Bathanti

> But I stay curved against the back
> of my sleeping wife in the bed
> I slept in as a boy —
>
> now the sewing room
> where my mother's beloved Singer
> that's done so much to cripple her dwells.
>
> The stairs try to throw her off their backs
> as she wills herself up them,
> through our door, and crimps
>
> over my wife, and I pretending to sleep,
> smoothing over us in this dark
> the quilt she herself spun.

EGGPLANT

So many times I've witnessed this
that *familiarity* is not the word

to conjure my mother's taking up of the breast-
shaped purple blackness, her paring

knife commencing from the areola,
strokes of peel stripping away into the sink

until the corpuscular fruit is nude
and ready to be sliced. In the colander

she tiers the rounds, salting each layer
to draw out the bitter water, and weights

them down with a piece of heart-
shaped iron with which her tailor father pressed.

They sit on the counter all day:
the eggplant with the heart pressing on them,

the water in the pan beneath
turning red.

Joseph Bathanti

For My Mother on Her 76th Birthday

Entering the airport terminal
we pass under the greening
statue of Charlotte, the city's namesake,
more tire-woman than queen,
grackles gripped on her bodice
as she tries to not blow away.

One of her bad mornings
my mother is having, the knotted
spine skewering her, nape
to crotch, cross-bones tirling
within her like sharpened sticks.

She's acceded to the gait of her forebears,
brick and needle-men, pain
not to be mentioned.
She walks as though something
from the other side is tugging her,
as if out of habit she must keep up,
but the effort is not worth it.

Strangers rush through the concourse,
impervious to one another
as if to look would be to recognize

oneself in that shoe or trench coat,
hatbox; that stooped pleated neck,
certain scent or inflection of the man
on the phone digging wildly in his pockets.

We pass them all, gate by gate,
leave them to their secrets;
there's nothing we can do about their lives.
What we all fear is our capricious bodies,
the mind's pigheaded fictions
like remnants in a consignment shop.

There comes a point in our farewell
when my mother is about to cry.
We forestall this moment with optimism:
Haven't we had a good time? Yes.
The children are adorable. Of course,
we'll see you at Thanksgiving.
The weather's been gorgeous.

Finally she gives in.
There's a softening in her voice,
a chink as momentary
as an interstice
in a second hand's revolution.
She touches my face,
an instinct drawn out by the end.

Joseph Bathanti

    Then she limps into the accordioned sleeve
    leading to the fuselage,
    a burst of incandescence
    enveloping her
    in its ephemera.

The Orange

In the acetylene light he is smoke,
wires and oddments splicing him
to the arithmetic of his unsuspected self:
02 SAT, blood pressure, pulse rate,

all in their turns blinking red,
bleating, chapter and verse,
in the electric book above his head.
Out of his shift coils a morphine epidural,

his face the color of eggplant,
two-prong oxygen cannula
like tusks where his teeth had been, hands
and feet exaggerating themselves with edema.

He wears a skullcap of flesh,
the same his father wore at 94,
the one he'll bequeath me,
the one I will leave mine.

A single orange flickers on the bedside table.
Seven stories below, beyond
the window in which he sits,
the wide and green Monongahela crawls,

Joseph Bathanti

    her shoulders draped in bridges,
    the only steel, now that the mills
    have died, on the river these days.
    From the other side of the water,

    a ruined church and a hill
    of abandoned union houses stare.
    There is one screamer on the unit.
    Like the man in the front car

    of a runaway roller coaster,
    he melds *stop* and *yay*, every few seconds,
    into a single screeching phoneme.
    The others, cuffed to trapezes,

    swaddle like mummies,
    their arms and legs, Xs and Ts,
    crooked at outlandish angles.
    The spinals totter in haloes,

    medieval chandeliers lashed to their heads.
    My father is such a practical man,
    I assume so unimaginative.
    What must he think – remanded

to this underworld – reduced now
like an immigrant to monosyllables?
We pet him.
I read him the sports page.

He never tells us to go away,
that he is scared and in pain.
More than anything he is surprised
that he has been left behind,

that what happened happened
in his sleep behind the wheel
of his new Buick Regal.
How unlike him to falter.

But now, the last millwright,
he refuses sleep,
will not even lie down,
but keeps vigil at the glass all night,

counting barge lights on the slow river,
holding in his giant hands the burning
orange he's saved to give my little boy
when he sees him again.

Practicing Love

Prince Street's been bulldozed,
the old neighborhood gone to hell.
You cannot sleep, Mother,
your head filled with News and cop shows,
mouthful of God. The boogie man
you desisted for me exhumes himself,
the mirrors grown infirm.

Before these streets were murderous,
I trotted them home, blue
to my knees from the principal's switch,
intent upon falling apart when I saw you;
but didn't. You never complained.
Silence, our best occasion,
I held my hands under scalding
water while you cleaned
the already immaculate house.

Nights, I made up reasons to cry out.
There was a piece of yellow wool
you'd lay across my stomach
when I could not sleep,
and tell me to say *a few prayers*.
Barely able to spell, The Hail Mary to me
sounded like the Lord's name in vain.

Now you invent reasons to call me.
I check the locks, watch until
the stranger passing is out of sight,
practice love, promising
to go back to church.
I never could tell the truth.
Your endearments break me.

Joseph Bathanti

Bitter

Knowing these days it takes a while
for my mother to get to the phone,
I let it ring and ring until she answers.

It's an accommodation
we've silently agreed upon.
Her voice, with the accent on *hell*

in *hello*, has not changed
in the fifty years I've known her.
It still delights me, in that first instant

before she knows who's calling,
when the world still holds promise.
But often enough the news is bad.

I am calling to find out
the arrangements for Nicky.
"How's Phyllis?" I ask.

"Skinny as a rail. I don't know
what she's going to do in that big house."
I don't know either,

so I inquire about the weather.
The temperature in Pittsburgh is nine degrees,
the biggest snowstorm in five years expected.

"It's so bitter," she sighs.
Because of the cold, my father does his walking
in the long halls of the big apartment

complex they moved to when they started
getting old and the neighborhood
and the house on Mellon Street, where I grew up,

got to be too much for them.
Last week, he caught his hand
in one of the building's heavy steel doors,

and broke a bone in it.
The hand turned black, but he waited
five days before going to the doctor

where all they did was put it in a brace.
Still, he can't get a glove on,
and it's minus-28 with the wind-chill.

To warm the hand, he draws it into his sleeve.
This morning, they went out to buy mittens,
but everyone was sold out.

Joseph Bathanti

My mother declares
that from one of my father's wool socks,
she'll make a mitten for his bad hand.

"What's the difference," she says, and I agree,
picturing them in a blizzard,
fighting their way,

with the rest of my ancient family,
behind the casket, up the frozen
hills of Mount Carmel,

my eighty-five year old father,
broken hand in a sock, trying
to keep my mother from falling.

The Future

Upon marrying in 1947,
my father eyes a farm in Evans City,
well north of Pittsburgh, in Butler County:
eighty acres split among corn,

winter wheat, and black angus cows.
Bees. Grapes and fruit trees;
a pond, two barns, vegetable garden,
tractor and three storey house

with a nice porch shaded by walnut trees.
He knows nothing about farming; but a plain,
patient man, drawn to rote, he is unafraid
of what the earth hides and might render.

He plans to move his new bride up there
and start a big family. In the short run,
for the sake of money, he'll keep his job
as a laborer at the Edgar Thomson Works

where he's been since '43, making steel
for the war, and commute every day
the forty or so miles to the mill in Braddock,
pull his shift feeding coke to blast furnaces

Joseph Bathanti

    on the open hearth,
    hustle back to Evans City,
    farm a few hours after supper,
    then hit it double-hard on Saturday and Sunday.

    He doesn't have the $12,000,
    but figures to somehow borrow it.
    For my mother, however, a farm
    is childish caprice, the kind of lark

    a man unacquainted with himself might attempt.
    She can't bear the country:
    soles caked with manure, calving cows
    screaming in agony under those black high nights,

    coyotes pleading as though for her blood.
    She wants high heels, to ride the streetcar
    downtown to Gimbel's, go to the show.
    She wants neighbors. Not beholden to an earth

    where dirt goes unchecked like lice,
    a land undressed, the moon larcenous
    and sharp enough to shear a bed in half.
    Wraithed in an unhemmed dress of chaff,

she'll grow angular, mealy-mouthed,
hair like dried thistle,
shambling off through the interminable crop
after phantom children.

There probably isn't even a hospital or A&P.
Why not just take the banana boat back to Naples?
My father does not argue – neither
to make his point nor defend himself.

Lying on the white chenille spread,
next to his wife, a hand behind his head,
the other rolling a lit Camel between thumb and forefinger,
he kisses her.

She tells him to shave,
lowers the sash and snaps off the lamp.
My father does not get mad,
does not push it to the point where she says,

I'm not going.
He backs off well before that,
seeing in her a wildness.
Not abandon nor recklessness,

Joseph Bathanti

but the wild, unbridled fear of earth,
fear that seizes her hands and claws them
through her long wavy brown hair,
pours like lighter fluid

out of her red lipsticked mouth
or, even worse, sutures in silence
that same mouth for days, weeks –
not even to eat, barely to breathe.

He slides off the bed and walks outside,
lights another cigarette, sits on the stoop,
and thinks for a few minutes about a
life absolved of steel:

the yield of fertile loam.
In the morning he'll charge into white heat,
the first ten of ten thousand pounds of slag on his spade.
In the club-yard, across the street,

old Italian men, who know the future,
steal time from their wives,
drink wine and play bocce.
Stars like ash powder the sky.

Maria Rosalina

There is a moment Sunday,
an inexplicable instant of clarity
and purpose the dying often summon,
when my mother extends a hand through the mist,
lifts off her bed and makes for the kitchen.

On a marble slab, she mixes egg and flour,
salt and water, rolls flat the shroud of dough,
snips it into *tagliatelle,*
and covers it with a sheet.

Even the rain halts and the sun appears
to allow her passage into the garden
for Romas, parsley,
garlic and *basilico.*

So that when we tiptoe into the etherized hush
of my parents' apartment,
and the long afternoon of one breath
and then one breath less,
we smell the sauce and hear Connie Francis
from the stereo singing *Al Di La.*

Joseph Bathanti

In the dining room: long still-warm
loaves of *Siciliano;* china
stationed at each place for *primi, secondo,*
the unhurried, comforting office of the table;
light, as day latens, flaring
in pitchers of purple chianti.

Her back to us, my mother
stands over the stove. At her side,
my father grates the *Pecorino,*
parries our looks of astonishment with a smile:
he knew all along she'd snap out of it.

In the large silver pot
we have worshipped all our lives,
water with the pasta
roils like an oracle.

My mother peers into it, stirring;
then turns to greet us:
red apron, pearls, sweatpants,
old-fashioned ladies white tennis shoes.
Prophetically,
she elevates the wooden spoon.

Behind her, columns of steam
rise and roost
in her white hair
like little statues.

Joseph Bathanti

Domenico Giusseppe

Singled from the queue filing
through airport security,
my 90 year old father is fully cooperative,
even amiable; not even surprised, it seems,

that fate has tapped him on the shoulder
to answer for something he is innocent of.
Two uniformed buxom matrons,
coiled hair and black patent leather

Sam Browns, heart-shaped
silver badges, ask him
if he's accepted anything from strangers
since he's entered the terminal.

He assures them he never accepts things from strangers.
They study him as if his affability
is part of the ploy, a filament
wired to the bomb he'll trigger.

They prod over him an electric wand,
slip him out of his overcoat, shake his cane.
He smiles and calls them *young lady*.
He's ordered to remove his shoes,

a pair of white Addidas,
not a scuff upon them; and his hat,
an old brown fedora they flip over
and over and empty of its nothingness,

before patting him down like a convict,
armpits and crotch, sliding
their hands up and down his arms and legs,
each skeletal ridge and knob

as if by magic he might divide
and reveal the vault of Armageddon.
Suddenly my father is terrible as Isaiah.
Yet he remains smiling, even as they strip him,

tottering naked on bare yellow feet,
white hair smoking off his chest,
millwright's legs tungsten blue,
from him emanating an audible tick.

Then they peel him out of his skin,
jackknife him open:
sprung, mis-spliced wires,
capped sockets, taped frays –

Joseph Bathanti

    the mysterious circuitry of detonation.
    Still they don't find what they're searching for,
    and he can't remember
    where he's hidden it.

My Father's Hat

My father owned a soft brown fedora.
As a child, I loved

to smell the inside of it,
the satin-lined crown

with its coat of arms:
two winged gryphons clutching

between them a shield flourished
with *New York*, against which

crested the roof of his head;
then sealed with glassy

batting, as if chambered
within lay a secret reliquary:

the eye teeth of Aquinas,
the still beating heart

of Thomas à Becket,
some secret tithing me

as my father's son
to this sacred hat.

Joseph Bathanti

Restoring Sacred Art

We ease the statue out of the Chevy trunk.
Stiff as a mob hit, she smiles,
tattered robe *della robia*,
nimbus studded with a star tiara.
In her arms, the smirking Christ-
child is lean and grim, in one hand
a ball with a cross planted in it,
the other held up like a boy scout's pledge.

I grab his mother in a headlock.
Philip takes the feet;
and we shuffle down Liberty Avenue:
Saturday night, the bars' glass-brick
windows lit with neon Iron City Light beer signs,
one Italian joint after another,
the spires of Saint Joseph's Cathedral
shooting off into the sky like wild onions.

We set her down for a minute at the foot
of Phil's studio and light cigarettes.
Four flights, fifteen steps each, straight up.
She stands there on the sidewalk,
holding the baby, gazing at Saint Joe's,

The Catholic Store, Mineo's Pizza,
the halogens twirling off across
the Bloomfield Bridge toward the Bishop's house.

The kid doesn't like it: the thrum
and noise, the lights. He's lived
all his life in a church.
We hoist them again and begin the climb,
pausing at each landing to rest, and crack at Mary:
You've got to lose some weight.
Too many cannolis.
When are you going to exercise?
We offer her a smoke.

At the top, we wrestle her inside.
Phil turns on the light.
The baby has lost those two fingers;
only the thumb remains,
jutting out of the fist like a hitchhiker's.
He wants down. In the full light,
Mary is wan, tired, the smile thinning.
She has trouble holding her son.
Her eyes are wet; her lips quiver.

Joseph Bathanti

This is not unusual, my friend tells me,
gesturing about his workroom
where other virgin mothers,
nicked and beat-up, missing limbs and noses,
awaiting restoration,
hold tightly to their squirming children,
trying to hush them, their tears
like gravel hitting the linoleum.

Photo credit: Jan Hensely

JOSEPH BATHANTI is the author of five books of poetry: *Communion Partners*, *Anson County*, *The Feast of All Saints*, *This Metal* (nominated for the National Book Award), and *Land of Amnesia*. His first novel, *East Liberty*, won the 2001 Carolina Novel Award. His latest novel, *Coventry*, won the 2006 Novello Literary Award. His book of stories, *The High Heart*, won the 2006 Spokane Prize for Short Fiction. He is the recipient of Literature Fellowships from the North Carolina Arts Council in 1994 (poetry) and 2009 (fiction), the Sherwood Anderson Award, and many others. He teaches at Appalachian State University in Boone, North Carolina.

Special thanks to Thomas Cervone, Philip DeLucia, David Friday, Trisha Hadley, Stephen Murabito, John Paul Russo, Steven Swerdfeger and his wonderful Star Cloud Press, and Troy Tuttle and the Marketing Communications Department at Appalachian State University.

www.ingramcontent.com/pod-product-compliance
Lightning Source LLC
LaVergne TN
LVHW011425080426
835512LV00005B/264